That Bear is Back!

by Elizabeth Best
illustrated by Craig Smith

Harcourt Achieve

Rigby • Saxon • Steck-Vaughn

www.HarcourtAchieve.com
1.800.531.5015

Characters

Polar bear

Peter

Contents

3

Chapter 1

Under the Bed

Something growled. The growl came from under Peter's bed.

Peter's eyes flew open.

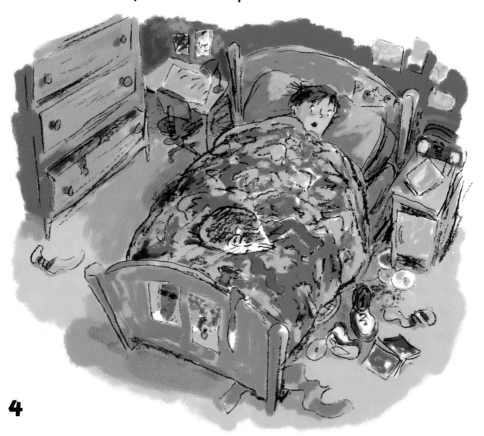

Peter knew that sound.

Last year Peter had found a polar bear in the fridge. The polar bear was eating hard-boiled eggs.

The polar bear liked Peter. He wanted
to keep Peter for a pet. It was terrible.

Peter told the bear that his sister
Matilda was big and fierce. That scared
the bear away.

Now the growl was back. Peter leaned over and looked under the bed.

That bear was back!

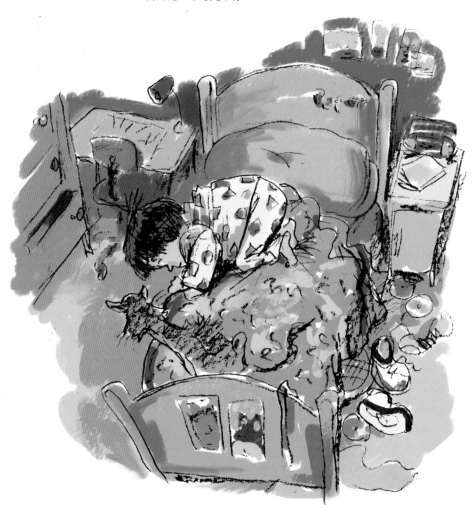

Peter's heart was beating fast. He crept out of bed and tiptoed toward the door. He decided to lock the bear in his bedroom and call the zoo.

Chapter 2

Orders

"Stop!" roared the bear.

Peter stopped.

"You told me a lie. You said that
Matilda was big," the bear roared.

Peter was shaking all over.

"She was big," said Peter, "but she . . .
she . . . she shrank."

"What made her shrink?" the bear asked.

Peter thought fast. "I made her shrink. I dipped her in shrinking powder."

"You're lying again," said the bear, resting on Peter's bed.

"Bring food!" shouted the bear. "Bring fish! Bring ice cream!"

"Push me on the swing," the bear
yelled. "Higher!"

14

"Wheel me in the baby carriage," the bear roared. "Faster!"

"Comb my hair! Brush my teeth!
Cut my toenails! Rub my back!"

At last the bear fell asleep.

Here was Peter's chance. He tiptoed to the phone.

Chapter 3

Bear Bath

"I have a very fine bear here," Peter whispered into the phone. "He's big and he's going cheap. In fact, you can have him for nothing."

Suddenly the bear was there. "Who's on the phone?" he roared.

"It's your wife," said Peter. "She wants you to go home."

"More lies!" roared the bear. "I have no wife."

"Look out!" cried Peter, pointing out the window. "Here comes Matilda."

The bear started to run. Then he remembered that Matilda wasn't big after all.

The bear stopped and looked. "She's cute," he said.

"Come into the yard and meet her," Peter said.

21

Peter had to get that bear outside.
Then he could run back into the house
and lock the door.

"What if she doesn't like me?" the
bear asked.

"Fill a bath for me!" the bear roared at Peter. "Icy-cold water! And soap! Lots of soap! I want to smell nice."

Peter had another idea. A great idea!

Chapter 4

Gone for Good

The bear was splashing around in the bath. Peter walked in with a paper bag full of powder.

Peter sprinkled the powder over the water.

"What's that?" asked the bear.

"It's shrinking powder!" said Peter with a smile.

With a terrible roar, the bear sprang out of the bath.

He shook water all over the bathroom.
He rolled on the floor like a wet dog.

He chased his tail. He ran in circles
until he was dizzy.

Then that polar bear ran out the front
door and was gone.

Peter smiled. Peter was sure that the bear was gone for good this time.

Glossary

crept
moved quietly and slowly

dizzy
a spinning feeling in your head

fierce
very tough

going cheap
selling something for a low price

gone for good
never coming back

growl
a low, angry noise

shrinking
making small

sprinkled
gently scattered

Elizabeth Best

This bear is a bully. I often think about bullies and wonder why they pick on other people.

In Australia, where I live, there's a game that children play . . . "If you don't do this or that, you have to be my servant for the whole day."

Are these children practicing to be bullies?

But . . . now I think about it . . . I wish I had someone who did everything I wanted for a whole day!

Craig Smith